Monetizing Your Passion: How to Turn Your Hobby into a Lucrative Income Stream

Coloring Ape

Published by Coloring Ape, 2023.

While every precaution has been taken in the preparation of this book, the publisher assumes no responsibility for errors or omissions, or for damages resulting from the use of the information contained herein.

MONETIZING YOUR PASSION: HOW TO TURN YOUR HOBBY INTO A LUCRATIVE INCOME STREAM

First edition. September 29, 2023.

Copyright © 2023 Coloring Ape.

ISBN: 979-8223457626

Written by Coloring Ape.

Table of Contents

Monetizing Your Passion:

How to Turn Your Hobby into a Lucrative Income Stream

In today's fast-paced world, many people dream of escaping the nine-to-five grind and pursuing their passions full-time. Whether it be painting, playing an instrument, or designing websites, turning a hobby into a lucrative income stream is becoming increasingly attractive. And why not? The idea of making money doing what you love sounds like a dream come true. But how can one actually monetize their passion effectively? In this article, we will delve into the strategies and steps you need to take in order to turn your hobby into a thriving business venture that not only allows you to express your creativity but also pays the bills. So if you're ready to make your dreams become a reality, keep reading as we show you how to unlock the potential within your favorite pastime and transform it into an income-generating machine.

Identifying Your Passion: Discovering what truly drives you

Discovering your passion is the first step towards turning it into a lucrative income stream. Here are some tips to help you identify what really drives you:

1. **Reflect on your interests and hobbies**: Take some time to think about activities that genuinely excite and motivate you. What do you enjoy doing in your free time? What topics or subjects intrigue you? These could be clues to uncovering your true passion.
2. **Consider your strengths and skills**: Assessing your strengths can also give insights into areas where you may have a natural inclination or talent. Think about the things at which people often praise you, as well as the tasks that come easily to you.
3. **Experiment with different experiences**: Don't limit yourself to just one field or hobby - try various activities! Engaging in new experiences allows for self-discovery and helps pinpoint specific interests that elicit enthusiasm from within.

Remember, monetizing a hobby requires genuine passion and dedication so ensure that whatever path chosen aligns with both personal enjoyment and market demand.

Assessing Market Demand: Finding out if your passion has profit potential

Assessing Market Demand

Before you dive headfirst into turning your hobby into a profitable income stream, it's important to assess the market demand for your product or service. This step will help you determine if there is a viable customer base that is willing to pay for what you have to offer.

1. **Research your target audience:** Start by identifying who your potential customers are and what they want or need. Conduct surveys, interviews, and online research to gather information about their preferences, purchasing behavior, and willingness to spend on products similar to yours.

2. **Analyze competitors:** Take a close look at other businesses or individuals offering similar products or services in the market. Understand their pricing strategies, marketing techniques, and customer reviews. This analysis will give you insights into how saturated the market is and if there is room for your offering.

3. **Test the demand:** Validate the potential demand for your product by conducting small-scale tests or creating prototypes that allow you to gauge customer interest before fully committing resources. Set up pre-orders or offer limited-time promotions to see how customers respond.

By thoroughly assessing market demand before pursuing monetization of your hobby, you can ensure that there is a viable target audience ready to support and pay for what you love doing most.

Building Your Personal Brand: Creating a strong and unique identity

- **Discover your unique qualities:** Reflect on what sets you apart from others in your hobby or industry. Identify your strengths, skills, and interests that make you stand out.

- **Craft a compelling narrative:** Develop a clear and concise story about who you are and what you offer. Highlight how your passion for your hobby drives your work and why people should choose to engage with you.

- **Be consistent across platforms:** Maintain a cohesive image by using the same logos, colors, fonts, and tone of voice across all online platforms. Consistency helps build recognition and trust among potential customers.

Optimize Your Online Presence: Amplifying reach through digital strategies

- **Create an engaging website or blog:** Establish an online hub where potential clients can learn more about you. Share high-quality content related to your hobby that showcases your expertise.

- **Leverage social media:** Utilize platforms such as Instagram, Facebook, Twitter, or TikTok to connect with a wider audience. Regularly post relevant content in order to build credibility and engagement.

- **Network strategically:** Attend industry events or join online communities where like-minded individuals gather. Make meaningful connections with influencers or professionals who can help promote your brand

Developing Your Skills: Honing your craft to stand out from the competition

Developing your skills: Honing your craft to stand out from the competition

1. Embrace continuous learning

To excel in monetizing your hobby, you must commit to constant skill development. Take advantage of workshops, classes, or online courses related to your passion. These educational opportunities will deepen your knowledge and help you stay up-to-date with industry trends.

2. Seek feedback and constructive criticism

Don't shy away from seeking feedback from experts or experienced professionals in your field. Their insights can provide valuable perspectives on enhancing your craft and refining your techniques. Constructive criticism may be tough to hear but is crucial for personal growth.

3. Experiment and innovate within boundaries

While staying true to the essence of what drew you towards pursuing a hobby professionally, don't hesitate to experiment and find innovative approaches that set you apart. This could involve trying new materials, incorporating technology advancements, or exploring fresh angles that capture attention.

4. Network strategically

Building a solid network within your niche community is essential for standing out in today's competitive landscape.To build connections effectively, don't just focus on self-promotion; strive to engage genuinely with like-minded individuals who share similar interests. You never know where opportunities might arise!

Creating a Business Plan: Mapping out your path to success

Before you start monetizing your passion, it's crucial to create a comprehensive business plan. This will serve as your roadmap, guiding you through the process of turning your hobby into a lucrative income stream.

1. **Define Your Goals**: Start by setting clear and specific goals for what you want to achieve with your hobby-turned-business. Are you looking to make a full-time income or supplement your existing job? Do you want to reach a certain number of customers or gain recognition in your industry? Knowing exactly what you're working towards will help shape the rest of your business plan.

2. **Identify Your Target Audience**: Understanding who your potential customers are is vital for marketing and sales strategies. Conduct thorough market research to identify their needs, preferences, and demographics. This information will enable you to tailor your products or services accordingly and position them effectively in the market.

3. **Develop a Marketing Strategy**: Once you have identified your target audience, it's time to create an effective marketing strategy that reaches them directly. Determine which channels (such as social media platforms or online marketplaces) are best suited for reaching and engaging with potential customers.

Remember: A well-thought-out business plan lays the foundation for success when monetizing your passion!

Finding Your Target Audience: Understanding who will pay for your passion

Understanding your target audience

Identifying who your target audience is crucial to monetizing your passion. Your target audience consists of individuals who will not only appreciate what you have to offer, but are also willing to pay for it. To understand your target audience better, it's important to conduct market research and gather data on demographics such as age, gender, location, and interests.

Tailoring your content

Once you have a clear understanding of your target audience, you can tailor your content specifically for them. By creating tailored content that resonates with their needs and preferences, you increase the chances of attracting their attention and keeping them engaged. Use language that they can relate to and address their pain points directly.

Building relationships through engagement

To effectively monetize your passion, building strong relationships with your target audience is essential. Engage with them through various channels such as social media platforms or email newsletters. Respond promptly to comments or messages and encourage feedback from them. This fosters a sense of trust and loyalty among your followers which can ultimately lead to conversions and increased revenue.

Setting Realistic Goals: Establishing achievable milestones for growth

Setting realistic goals is crucial when monetizing your passion and turning it into a lucrative income stream. By establishing achievable milestones, you can track your progress and stay motivated along the way.

1. Define your objectives: Start by clearly defining what you want to achieve with your hobby-turned-business. Whether it's earning a certain amount of money per month or reaching a specific number of clients, having clear objectives will help guide your actions.
2. Break it down: Once you have defined your main goal, break it down into smaller, more manageable milestones. These could be monthly or quarterly targets that align with your overall objective.
3. Be specific and measurable: Make sure each milestone is specific and measurable so that you can accurately track your progress. For example, instead of setting a vague goal like "increase sales," set a target such as "increase sales by 10% in the next three months."
4. Stay realistic: While it's important to challenge yourself, remember to set goals that are attainable within a reasonable timeframe. Unrealistic expectations can lead to frustration and disappointment.
5. Track Your Progress Efficiently- Regularly monitor how close or far away from achieving success you actually are using metrics specifically designed for this purpose. Empty recommends creating a dashboard measuring KPIs most vital for determining success on their platform. It's not just about tracking revenue;thereby mapping out everything trending across all channel growth. Take note. Monthly comparisons end up giving undue importance, right alongside an earlier determination. Bear in mind, digging deeper when necessary getting better results, cataloguing scrutinised elements. Sheer metrics do not make sense if there's no relation drawn towards associated costs. Invest time wisely. Remember, time equals money. Several different ways exist breaking pivotal information exactly into pieces meant for being closely attacked one move at any given moment. If doing application-

based marketing better dominate, advantages make themselves evident.

Pricing Your Products or Services: Determining the value of your passion

Determining the value of your passion

Are you ready to turn your hobby into a profitable business? One crucial step is pricing your products or services correctly. When determining the value of what you offer, consider factors like market demand, competition, and production costs.

Research market demand

Start by researching if there is a demand for what you are offering. Look for similar products or services in the market and analyze their popularity and customer reviews. This will help you gauge whether people are willing to pay for what you have to offer.

Analyze the competition

Study your competitors' pricing strategies carefully. Compare their prices with their product quality, features, and benefits provided. By understanding how they position themselves in the market, you can set competitive prices that differentiate your offering without undervaluing it.

Calculate production costs

To ensure profitability, calculate all aspects of production costs: materials, labor, overhead expenses, packaging, shipping fees – everything that goes into creating and delivering your product or service. Consider any ongoing expenses as well.

By considering these factors together – researching market demand while analyzing competition alongside calculating production costs -you will be better positioned to determine the optimal price point for monetizing on Your Passion successfully!

Building an Online Presence: Utilizing digital platforms to reach a wider audience

One of the key steps in monetizing your passion is building an online presence by leveraging various digital platforms. By doing so, you can expand your reach and attract a larger audience interested in what you have to offer.

- **Creating a Website:** Start by establishing a professional-looking website that showcases your expertise, products, or services. Make sure it is user-friendly and optimized for search engines so that potential customers can easily find you.

- **Engaging on Social Media:** Utilize social media platforms like Facebook, Twitter, and Instagram to connect with your target market. Regularly share valuable content related to your hobby or industry, engage with followers through comments and messages, and promote any special offers or events.

- **Starting a Blog/Vlog:** Consider starting a blog or vlog where you can share your knowledge and experiences within your niche. This not only establishes yourself as an authority but also gives people another reason to visit your website regularly.

Remember that consistency is key when building an online presence—regularly update your website/blog/vlog and interact with followers on social media platforms to maintain engagement levels. With time, these efforts will pay off as you attract more visitors who are eager to support and invest in monetizing their passions too!

Marketing and Promotion: Strategies to attract customers and increase visibility

When it comes to turning your hobby into a lucrative income stream, marketing and promotion are essential for attracting customers and increasing visibility. Here are some strategies to help you get started:

1. **Leverage social media:** Use platforms like Instagram, Facebook, and Twitter to showcase your work. Post high-quality photos or videos that highlight the unique features of your products or services. Interact with your audience through comments and messages to build relationships and generate interest.
2. **Create a website or blog:** Establishing an online presence is crucial in reaching a wider audience. Design an appealing website that showcases your portfolio or products in an organized manner. Incorporate relevant keywords into your content to improve search engine results.
3. **Collaborate with influencers:** Partnering with influencers who align with your niche can expose your brand to their followers, resulting in increased visibility and potential sales. Reach out to influencers by offering free samples or collaborations tailored specifically for them.
4. **Offer promotions:** Attract new customers by running promotions such as discounts, limited-time offers, or referral rewards programs. This not only encourages immediate sales but also generates buzz around your brand.

Remember that consistency is key when implementing these strategies—regularly update social media profiles, maintain a well-functioning website, nurture influencer relationships, and continuously evaluate the effectiveness of promotional tactics.

Leveraging Social Media: Harnessing the power of social networks for your business

Social media has transformed the way businesses operate, providing a powerful platform to promote and monetize hobbies. By strategically leveraging social media platforms such as Facebook, Instagram, and Twitter, individuals can reach a vast audience and turn their passion into a lucrative income stream.

- Build an engaging online presence: Establishing a strong brand identity on social media is crucial for attracting followers and potential customers. Create compelling content that showcases your hobby in unique ways and resonates with your target audience.

- Utilize influencer marketing: Partnering with influencers who align with your niche can significantly expand your reach and credibility. Collaborate with these personalities by offering them free products or services in exchange for promoting your brand to their existing fan base.

- Leverage user-generated content: Encourage followers to share their experiences with your hobby by hosting contests or challenges. User-generated content not only fosters community engagement but also serves as free advertising for your brand.

In conclusion, harnessing the power of social networks through strategic tactics like building an engaging online presence, utilizing influencer marketing, and leveraging user-generated content can help individuals effectively monetize their passions on social media platforms.

Networking and Collaborations: Connecting with like-minded individuals and businesses

Building a network of like-minded individuals and collaborating with businesses can be instrumental in turning your hobby into a lucrative income stream. By connecting with others who share your passion, you increase the opportunities for growth, learning, and exposure.

- Attend industry events or join online communities related to your hobby to meet people who are as enthusiastic about it as you are. These connections can lead to partnerships or mentorship opportunities.

- Reach out to local businesses that align with your interests. Offer collaborations such as joint promotions or product partnerships that benefit both parties involved.

- Leverage social media platforms to connect with potential collaborators or target customers. Engage in meaningful conversations, share valuable content, and promote each other's work.

Remember, networking is not just about getting something from others but also giving back by supporting their endeavors. Nurture these relationships by actively engaging with fellow hobbyists and being open to new ideas and possibilities.

Diversifying Income Streams: Exploring different ways to make money from your passion

Exploring Different Ways to Make Money from Your Passion

1. Freelancing

If you have a passion for writing, graphic design, programming, or any other marketable skill, consider freelancing as a way to monetize your passion. Freelancing allows you to work on projects that align with your interests while earning income. You can find freelance opportunities through online platforms and build a portfolio of your work to attract clients.

2. Creating Digital Products

Another lucrative option is creating and selling digital products related to your passion. Whether it's an e-book, online course, or downloadable artwork, digital products provide the opportunity for passive income as customers can purchase them repeatedly without requiring additional production costs.

3. Offering Services or Coaching

If you enjoy teaching and helping others succeed in their journey related to your passion, offering services or coaching can be profitable avenues. For example, if you're passionate about fitness and wellness, offer personal training sessions or create customized workout plans for clients.

By diversifying your income streams using these approaches along with others specific to your field of interest such as product endorsements or affiliate marketing partnerships), you can turn what once was just a hobby into a lucrative source of income!

Creating a Profitable Online Course: Sharing your expertise and monetizing it

Identify Your Expertise

To create a profitable online course, start by identifying your expertise. What knowledge or skills do you possess that others might find valuable? Consider your hobbies, work experience, or educational background as potential areas of expertise.

Define Your Target Audience

Once you've identified your expertise, define your target audience. Who would benefit most from the knowledge you have to share? Determine their age range, interests, and skill levels to tailor your course content accordingly.

Develop Engaging Content

Next, develop engaging content for your online course. Break down complex information into digestible units and use multimedia elements like videos or interactive quizzes to enhance learning. Keep in mind that clear communication is key – use simple language without jargon or technical terms.

Choose a Platform

Selecting the right platform is crucial for success when creating an online course. Research different options such as e-learning platforms or video hosting websites like YouTube. Consider factors such as user-friendly interfaces, payment processing capabilities, and support resources offered by each platform.

Market Your Course

To monetize your passion successfully through an online course requires effective marketing strategies. Leverage social media platforms relevant to your target audience to promote the course's benefits and generate interest.

Turning Your Passion into a Book: Publishing your knowledge and experiences

Writing a book is a great way to monetize your passion and share your knowledge or experiences. Here are some steps to get started:

- **Identify your niche**: Determine the specific topic or theme that sets you apart from other books in the market.

- **Create an outline**: Organize your thoughts and ideas into an outline, which will act as a roadmap for writing your book.

- **Research and gather information**: Conduct thorough research to ensure that the content of your book is accurate, reliable, and up-to-date.

- **Write consistently**: Set aside dedicated time each day or week to write, ensuring steady progress towards completing your manuscript.

- **Edit and revise**: After finishing the first draft, review it multiple times for grammar, clarity, and overall coherence.

- **Find professional editing services**: Consider hiring an editor who can provide valuable feedback and help polish your manuscript before publishing.

Publishing Options: There are several avenues available when it comes to publishing your book:

- Traditional Publishing: Submitting manuscripts to established publishers can be competitive but offers wider distribution potential if accepted. However, it may involve surrendering some creative control.

- Self-Publishing: With self-publishing platforms like Amazon Kindle Direct Publishing (KDP) or Smashwords, you have full control over the process. This option allows for higher royalties but requires more effort in marketing and promotion.

Remember that consistency is key during this entire process—both in writing regularly and diligently following through on publication efforts. Through determination and persistence on turning their passion into a lucrative income stream by transforming their hobby into published works authors could increase their chances of success.

Licensing and Merchandising: Expanding your brand through merchandise and licensing deals

Utilizing Licensing and Merchandising to Expand Your Brand

One effective way to turn your hobby into a lucrative income stream is by exploring licensing and merchandising opportunities. By leveraging your brand through merchandise and licensing deals, you can reach a wider audience and generate additional revenue.

Merchandising involves creating products related to your hobby, such as t-shirts, mugs, or accessories that feature your unique designs or logos. These items can be sold online on platforms like Etsy or through your own website. Licensing entails granting permission for other companies to use your brand on their products in exchange for royalties or fees.

Here are some key considerations when venturing into licensing and merchandising:

1. **Protecting Your Intellectual Property**: Before moving forward with any licensing agreements, it's crucial to secure copyright or trademark protection for your brand. This ensures that others cannot profit from copying or imitating your work without authorization.
2. **Choosing the Right Partners**: When selecting partners for merchandise collaboration or licensees, carefully assess their reputation, target market alignment, distribution channels, and track record of successfully launching similar products.
3. **Maximizing Reach**: Look beyond traditional brick-and-mortar retailers by considering e-commerce platforms like Amazon Marketplace or partnering with influencers who can promote your merchandise on social media.

By strategically leveraging licensing and merchandising opportunities aligned with their passion projects, individuals can transform hobbies into profitable ventures while simultaneously increasing brand awareness among an expanded customer base.

Setting Up a Physical Store or Studio: Taking your passion offline and into the real world

When it comes to turning your hobby into a profitable business, one option is to set up a physical store or studio. This allows you to showcase and sell your products or services in person, providing a personal touch that online platforms can't replicate.

- Find the perfect location for your store or studio. Consider factors such as foot traffic, accessibility, and target audience demographics.

- Create an inviting atmosphere by designing a layout that reflects your brand identity and ensures ease of browsing for customers.

- Invest in quality fixtures and displays that highlight the uniqueness of your products or services.

- Build relationships with suppliers to ensure consistent inventory and reliable delivery of goods.

- Implement effective marketing strategies through signage, local advertising, partnerships with neighboring businesses, and hosting events or workshops.

Elevate customer experience through exceptional service

In addition to showcasing your passion through an appealing physical space, it's crucial to prioritize customer satisfaction. Providing excellent service will not only keep customers coming back but also generate positive word-of-mouth recommendations:

- Train friendly and knowledgeable staff who can assist customers with their inquiries or help them make informed purchasing decisions.

● Offer personalized recommendations based on each customer's preferences and needs.

● Provide flexible payment options such as cash, credit cards, mobile payment apps like Apple Pay or Google Pay, etc., to cater to different customer preferences.

● Develop loyalty programs that reward repeat customers with exclusive discounts or early access to new products.

By setting up a physical store or studio, you create opportunities for direct interaction with customers while establishing yourself as a trusted expert in your field.

Building a Team: Delegating tasks to scale your business

To effectively monetize your passion and turn it into a lucrative income stream, it's essential to build a strong team and delegate tasks appropriately. By sharing the workload, you can free up time and energy for more important aspects of growing your business.

1. Identify your strengths and weaknesses:

Take an honest evaluation of your skills and determine where you excel as well as areas that could benefit from additional support. This self-awareness will allow you to assign tasks more strategically by delegating those that align with others' strengths.

1. Hire specialists:

Consider bringing in experts who have specialized knowledge or experience in particular areas that require attention. This might include marketing, social media management, customer service, or product development. Leveraging their expertise will not only enhance the quality of work but also save you valuable time.

1. Establish clear roles and responsibilities:

Clearly define each team member's role within the business and outline their specific responsibilities to ensure accountability and efficiency. Document these details in job descriptions or agreements so that everyone is on the same page about their duties.

4-5 additional steps should follow below this paragraph.

- Communicate effectively: Regularly communicate with your team members, providing them with updates on projects or changes in expectations.

● Trust your team: Delegate decision-making authority whenever possible to empower individual team members' growth while alleviating pressure from yourself.

● Foster collaboration: Encourage teamwork among employees, fostering an environment where ideas can be freely shared, allowing for innovation. By implementing these practices into building an effective team through delegation selection strategies when necessary; one ensures scalability overtime because success relies heavily upon the efforts invested collectively rather than individually alone

Overcoming Challenges and Obstacles: Strategies to navigate the ups and downs of entrepreneurship

Strategies for Overcoming Challenges and Obstacles in Entrepreneurship

1. Embrace a growth mindset: Developing a growth mindset is crucial when navigating the ups and downs of entrepreneurship. Instead of viewing obstacles as failures, see them as opportunities to learn and grow. Recognize that setbacks are part of the journey towards success.
2. Seek support from mentors: Building relationships with experienced entrepreneurs who have overcome similar challenges can provide valuable guidance and insights. Reach out to mentors who can offer advice, share their experiences, and help you navigate through difficult times.
3. Stay focused on your goals: As an entrepreneur, it's easy to get overwhelmed by day-to-day tasks or external distractions. Create a clear vision for your business and set specific goals that align with your passion monetization strategies. This will help keep you motivated during challenging times.
4. Develop problem-solving skills: Entrepreneurs often face unexpected challenges unique to their businesses - this requires adaptable thinking along side strong innovative instincts; focus must be placed finding alternative solutions rather than dwelling too long any difficulties occurred.

Additional Tips:

- Build a strong network by attending industry events or joining local entrepreneurial communities.

- Take care of yourself physically and mentally by setting boundaries, staying organized, practicing self-care.

- Continuous learning is key; stay updated with industry trends & innovations to adapt accordingly improve decision making process By implementing these strategies, entrepeneurships become equipped developeding agile confident mindsets enabling empowering overcoming obstacles successfully while pivoting adapting emergent information availablegic responses+From building relationships seeking continual personal professional development protect ensures sustainable healthier mental wellbeing aid innovation profitability

Scaling Your Passion Business: Growing your venture to new heights

Once you have successfully monetized your passion and established a steady income stream, it's essential to think about scaling your business for continued growth. Here are a few key strategies to take your venture to new heights:

1. **Expand Your Reach**: Consider reaching out beyond your current customer base by exploring different marketing channels such as social media advertising and influencer partnerships. This will help you tap into new markets and attract a larger audience.

2. **Diversify Your Offerings**: To increase revenue streams, consider expanding the range of products or services you offer. This can involve creating complementary merchandise, offering online courses or workshops related to your hobby, or even branching out into consulting or coaching services.

3. **Streamline Operations**: As your passion business grows, efficiency becomes crucial for sustained success. Look for ways to automate processes, delegate tasks where necessary, and implement systems that allow for scalability without sacrificing quality.

Remember that scaling a passion-based business takes time and careful planning - don't rush the process in pursuit of quick profits! Focus on building strong foundations while remaining true to what initially sparked your interest in this venture.

Unlocking Entrepreneurship: 10 Lucrative Business Models to Launch on a Shoestring Budget

In today's highly competitive business landscape, aspiring entrepreneurs often face one significant obstacle: the lack of financial resources to get their ventures off the ground. However, with the right mindset and a dash of creativity, launching a lucrative business on a shoestring budget is not only possible but also immensely rewarding. This article delves into ten innovative and proven business models that can unlock entrepreneurial success without breaking the bank. From e-commerce platforms to subscription services and freelancing opportunities, these cost-effective strategies offer an abundance of potential for ambitious individuals willing to think outside the box. So if you're ready to dive headfirst into entrepreneurship without draining your savings account, read on as we explore how these ten profitable ventures can be launched with minimal capital investment but maximum return on investment.

E-commerce platforms: Capitalizing on the booming online retail market

E-commerce platforms have emerged as a lucrative business model for entrepreneurs looking to capitalize on the growing trend of online shopping. With low startup costs and the ability to reach a global audience, these platforms provide an accessible entry point into the world of entrepreneurship.

- Online retail market boom: The rise in e-commerce has been fueled by changing consumer preferences and advancements in technology. More people than ever before are turning to online shopping, creating a massive opportunity for entrepreneurs to tap into this market.

- Low barriers to entry: Setting up an e-commerce platform requires minimal investment compared to traditional brick-and-mortar stores. With affordable website builders and easy-to-use payment gateways, launching an online store has become simplified even for those with limited technical knowledge.

- Global reach: Unlike physical stores that are confined to local markets, e-commerce platforms can attract customers from around the world. This global reach allows entrepreneurs to scale their businesses quickly and access diverse customer bases.

The appeal of e-commerce platforms is undeniable, offering aspiring entrepreneurs a chance to enter the thriving online retail market with minimal resources and maximum growth potential.

Subscription services: Generating recurring revenue with a small initial investment

Subscription services offer a lucrative business model that allows entrepreneurs to generate recurring revenue with minimal upfront costs. Here's why this model can be a game-changer for those looking to launch on a shoestring budget:

1. **Low overhead costs:** With subscription services, entrepreneurs can leverage existing resources and infrastructure, reducing the need for substantial upfront investments in inventory or physical store space.
2. **Predictable cash flow:** The recurring nature of subscription payments provides businesses with a steady stream of income, making it easier to forecast future revenues and allocate resources effectively.
3. **Customer loyalty:** By offering valuable products or services at an affordable monthly fee, subscription businesses can foster long-term relationships with customers, leading to repeat purchases and increased customer lifetime value.
4. **Scalability:** As your subscriber base grows, so does your revenue potential without proportionally increasing operational costs. This scalability allows for rapid growth while maintaining profitability.
5. **Flexible pricing models:** Subscription services provide entrepreneurs with the flexibility to test different pricing strategies and offerings to find what resonates best with their target audience.

In summary, subscription services present an attractive business model that generates predictable revenue streams while requiring limited initial capital investment. This has made it increasingly popular among entrepreneurs looking to unlock entrepreneurship opportunities on even the tightest budgets.

Freelancing opportunities: Leveraging your skills to offer services on a flexible basis

Freelancing has become an increasingly popular way for professionals to leverage their skills and earn income on a flexible basis. With the rise of remote work and digital platforms, freelancers can now offer their services to clients around the world from the comfort of their own homes. This business model allows entrepreneurs to tap into their expertise and create a thriving business with minimal startup costs.

Advantages of freelancing

- Flexibility: One of the biggest advantages of freelancing is the ability to work on your own terms. You can choose when, where, and how much you want to work, allowing for a better work-life balance.

- Low overhead costs: Unlike traditional businesses, freelancers don't have high overhead costs like rent or inventory. All you need is a computer and internet connection to start offering your services.

- Diverse client base: As a freelancer, you have the opportunity to work with clients from various industries and locations. This not only keeps your work interesting but also helps expand your professional network.

Finding freelance opportunities

- Online marketplaces: There are numerous online platforms like Upwork and Fiverr that connect freelancers with potential clients. These platforms provide visibility and access to a large pool of potential clients.

- Networking events: Attending industry-specific conferences or networking events can help you meet potential clients face-to-face. Building personal connections can lead to long-term partnerships.

- Referrals: Satisfied clients can be an excellent source of referrals for new projects. Maintaining good relationships with your existing clients is crucial for generating repeat business as well as getting recommended by them.

By leveraging your skills as a freelancer, you have the opportunity to create a lucrative business model without breaking the bank. With flexibility in schedule and low upfront costs, this entrepreneurial path offers great potential for success in today's digital age.

Dropshipping: Partnering with suppliers to sell products without inventory costs

Dropshipping is a business model that allows entrepreneurs to sell products online without the need for large upfront inventory costs. Instead of purchasing and storing products, dropshippers partner with suppliers who ship the products directly to the customers' doorsteps. This eliminates the need for warehousing and shipping logistics, making it an attractive option for those on a shoestring budget.

With dropshipping, entrepreneurs can focus on building their brand and marketing their store while leaving the operations aspect to their suppliers. This allows them to start their business quickly and efficiently. Additionally, since they only pay for the product after it has been sold, there is minimal financial risk involved.

Advantages of dropshipping include:

- Low startup costs: Unlike traditional retail businesses that require significant investment in inventory upfront, dropshipping requires little capital as you don't have to purchase any stock before selling.

- Easy scalability: With no constraints related to storage space or handling logistics yourself, scaling your dropshipping business can be seamless.

- Wider product range: As you are not limited by physical space or warehouse size restrictions when using a third-party supplier's inventory, you can offer a wide variety of niche products in your online store.

By leveraging strategic partnerships with reliable suppliers through dropshipping arrangements, entrepreneurs have an opportunity to unlock profitability even on limited budgets.

Affiliate marketing: Promoting other businesses' products and earning commissions

One lucrative business model that requires minimal investment is affiliate marketing. This involves promoting other businesses' products or services on your website or social media platforms and earning a commission for each sale made through your unique referral link.

With affiliate marketing, you don't need to create your own product, deal with inventory management, or handle customer service - making it relatively easy to startup compared to other business models.

To get started, you simply need to find an affiliate program that aligns with your niche or target audience. Many companies offer such programs and provide promotional materials like banners or text links for their affiliates. By strategically placing these promotions in front of your audience, you can generate passive income while building rapport with potential customers for the company you are promoting.

Affiliate marketing offers a flexible way to earn money online without the traditional burdens of running a brick-and-mortar business. It allows individuals looking to launch a venture on a limited budget access to potentially high-profit opportunities in diverse niches ranging from beauty and health products to technology gadgets and software solutions.

Online courses and coaching: Sharing expertise and knowledge for a fee

Online courses and coaching have emerged as highly lucrative business models that can be launched on a shoestring budget. Entrepreneurs with specialized skills or knowledge can leverage the power of the internet to reach a global audience, offering their expertise at a fee.

Advantages of online courses and coaching:

- Flexibility: Online courses allow entrepreneurs to create content once and sell it repeatedly, providing flexibility in terms of time management.

- Scalability: By leveraging digital platforms, entrepreneurs are able to scale their businesses rapidly without incurring significant additional costs.

- Accessible pricing: With low overhead costs associated with traditional brick-and-mortar establishments, online course creators can offer their valuable information at affordable prices while still generating substantial profits.

Tips for success:

1. Identify your target audience: Understanding who will benefit most from your knowledge is crucial for developing relevant content.
2. Create high-quality content: Invest time and effort into creating comprehensive materials that deliver real value to your students or clients.
3. Leverage social media marketing strategies: Utilize platforms like Instagram or LinkedIn to promote your services, connect with potential customers, and build credibility within your industry.

Overall, launching an online course or coaching business offers aspiring entrepreneurs an opportunity to share their expertise while generating revenue even on a tight budget. Through careful planning and strategic execution, these ventures hold immense potential for financial success.

Social media consulting: Helping businesses optimize their online presence

Social Media Consulting: Helping businesses optimize their online presence

In today's digital age, having a strong online presence is crucial for the success of any business. However, navigating the complexities of social media can be overwhelming and time-consuming. That's where social media consulting comes in.

A social media consultant works closely with businesses to develop and implement effective strategies to optimize their online presence. By conducting market research and analyzing target audiences, they create tailored content that resonates with customers. They also monitor and analyze engagement metrics to help businesses stay ahead of trends and adapt their strategies accordingly.

With their expertise in various platforms such as Facebook, Instagram, Twitter, LinkedIn, and YouTube, social media consultants ensure that businesses make the most out of each platform by reaching the right audience at the right time. Whether it is creating eye-catching visuals or crafting compelling captions, these professionals know how to capture attention and drive user engagement.

By partnering with a social media consultant on a shoestring budget, entrepreneurs can unlock new opportunities for growth without breaking the bank or diverting resources from other critical areas of their business. With this cost-effective solution, businesses can build brand awareness, attract new customers, and achieve long-term success in the competitive landscape of today's digital marketplace.

Content creation: Producing valuable and engaging content for businesses

Content Creation: Producing Valuable and Engaging Content for Businesses

In today's digital age, businesses need to establish a strong online presence to thrive. One of the most effective ways to achieve this is through creating valuable and engaging content. Whether it's blog posts, social media updates, or videos, high-quality content attracts potential customers and keeps them coming back for more.

The power of well-crafted content

Content creation allows businesses to showcase their expertise in a particular field. By sharing informative articles or insightful videos, they can position themselves as industry leaders while building trust with their target audience. Furthermore, great content has the potential to go viral and be shared across various platforms, expanding reach on a limited budget.

How to create compelling content on a shoestring budget

1. Research your target audience: Understanding what type of content resonates with your audience is vital. Conduct surveys or analyze data from social media insights tools to discover their preferences and interests.
2. Focus on quality over quantity: Instead of churning out mediocre content daily, invest time in creating original pieces that provide value.
3. Leverage user-generated content: Encourage customers to share their experiences by featuring testimonials or running contests where users submit creative materials related to your brand.
4. Collaborate with influencers: Team up with influencers who align with your business values and have engaged followership – they can amplify your message without breaking the bank.

Remember that producing valuable and engaging content takes time—don't rush the process just because you're working within limitations. With consistent effort and creativity, even entrepreneurs operating on shoestring budgets can develop impactful digital marketing strategies through compelling storytelling techniques via different forms of media such as writing/blogging (e. g., SEO-friendly website copy), video production/animations (e. g., YouTube channels), graphic design/infographics (e. g., Pinterest boards) etcetera which will help boost customer acquisition rates while keeping existing customers engaged and satisfied.

Virtual assistant services: Providing administrative support remotely

● In today's digital age, virtual assistant services have become increasingly popular among entrepreneurs looking for cost-effective ways to manage their businesses.

● Virtual assistants are skilled professionals who provide administrative support remotely, helping entrepreneurs with tasks such as scheduling appointments, managing emails, and creating documents.

● Hiring a virtual assistant can be an affordable alternative to hiring an in-house employee, as it eliminates the need for office space and equipment expenses.

Print-on-demand: Selling custom-designed products without inventory expenses

E-commerce has opened up opportunities for entrepreneurs to sell their own unique designs on various products without the need for inventory. With print-on-demand services, you can create and sell custom-designed t-shirts, hoodies, mugs, and more, all without having to invest in bulk quantities of product upfront.

Here's how it works:

1. Upload your design: Create a captivating and original design that resonates with your target audience.
2. Choose your product: Select from a wide range of items such as clothing, accessories, or home decor that can be customized with your design.
3. Set up your online store: Utilize e-commerce platforms like Shopify or Etsy to set up an online store where customers can browse and purchase your products.
4. Fulfillment made easy: When an order is placed on your website, the print-on-demand service will handle all aspects of production and shipping directly to the customer.

Print-on-demand allows entrepreneurs to focus on creating unique designs while outsourcing production logistics. This business model reduces financial risks by eliminating the need for purchasing large amounts of inventory upfront—making it an ideal choice for those launching a business with limited capital.

App development: Creating and selling mobile applications

1. **Lucrative business model:** Develop, market, and sell mobile applications to users worldwide.

○ With the increasing popularity of smartphones, there is a growing demand for innovative and user-friendly apps.

○ Mobile app stores provide developers with a platform to reach millions of potential customers.

2. **Low budget requirements:** Building a successful app doesn't have to break the bank.

○ Basic programming skills are essential but can be self-taught or acquired through affordable online courses.

○ Free resources like open-source frameworks, libraries, and design templates can help keep costs down.

3. **Monetization strategies for sustained profits:**

● In-app purchases: Offer extra features or content that users can unlock by making purchases within the app.

● Advertising revenue: Integrate ads into the app to generate income from advertisers who want to reach your user base.

1. **Key considerations for success in app development:**

● Market research is crucial – identify popular niche markets and target specific user needs rather than trying to be everything for everyone.

● Create an appealing user interface (UI) that is intuitive and visually attractive – this will increase downloads and positive reviews.

In conclusion, tapping into the lucrative field of app development offers great potential while requiring minimal initial investment. By focusing on niche markets, providing value-added features/content, using effective monetization strategies, and delivering a visually pleasing UI experience; entrepreneurs can create highly profitable mobile applications even with limited resources.

Digital marketing agency: Assisting businesses with online marketing strategies

A digital marketing agency specializes in helping businesses develop effective online marketing strategies. These agencies have the expertise to create and implement digital campaigns across various channels, such as social media, search engines, and email. They understand the latest trends in consumer behavior and use data analytics to optimize campaigns for maximum impact.

Benefits of hiring a digital marketing agency include:

- Increased visibility: A well-executed digital strategy can help businesses reach their target audience more effectively, increasing brand awareness and visibility.

- Enhanced customer engagement: By leveraging various online platforms, a digital marketing agency can help businesses connect with customers on a deeper level through personalized messaging and interactive content.

- Improved ROI: With their knowledge of ad targeting techniques and data-driven insights, a professional agency can ensure that every advertising dollar is spent wisely, maximizing return on investment.

Choosing the right digital marketing agency is crucial for entrepreneurs looking to make an impact without breaking the bank. Researching different agencies' track records, evaluating their past campaigns' success rates, and requesting proposals are all steps that aspiring business owners should take before selecting an agency to partner with.

Event planning: Organizing events on a small budget for clients

Planning and organizing events can be a lucrative business model that doesn't require a huge initial investment. Here are some tips to successfully launch this venture even with limited funds:

1. **Focus on niche markets**: Targeting specific industries or interest groups allows you to tailor your event planning services and reach potential clients more effectively.
2. **Collaborate with local vendors**: Building relationships with nearby suppliers, caterers, and venues can lead to cost-saving partnerships and favorable discounts.
3. **Maximize digital marketing**: Utilize social media platforms, email newsletters, and online advertisements to promote your event planning services without the need for expensive advertising campaigns.
4. **Optimize resources through outsourcing**: Instead of hiring full-time staff, consider outsourcing tasks such as graphic design or content creation to freelancers who specialize in those areas.

By implementing these strategies and being resourceful, you can excel in event planning while operating within a small budget.

Home-based food business: Starting a catering or baking business from home

Starting a catering or baking business from the comfort of your own kitchen is an excellent option for aspiring entrepreneurs on a tight budget. With the rise in demand for personalized and quality food services, there are plenty of opportunities to thrive in this competitive industry.

Here are a few important considerations when starting your home-based food business:

1. **Food safety regulations**: It's essential to familiarize yourself with local health department requirements and obtain any necessary permits or licenses before launching your venture.
2. **Specialization**: Decide whether you want to focus on catering events, providing baked goods, or both. Specializing can help you target specific customer segments and stand out in the market.
3. **Promotion**: Leverage social media platforms like Facebook and Instagram to showcase your delectable creations visually, attract customers through word-of-mouth referrals, and build your brand reputation.
4. **Pricing strategy**: Determine how much it costs to create each dish including ingredients, packaging materials, and labor hours then set prices that allow for profit while keeping them attractive compared to competitors'. 5.**Networking:** Collaborating with wedding planners, event venuesand other industry professionals is vitalfor attracting clientsand building connections.

By leveraging creativity, true passion for cooking, a solid work ethic, and constant improvement, you can turnyour loveoffoodinto asuccessfulhomebasedbusinessventure!

Personal styling and image consulting: Helping individuals enhance their personal brand

- A great business idea for entrepreneurs on a tight budget is to offer personal styling and image consulting services.

- By helping individuals enhance their personal brand, you can provide guidance on clothing choices, grooming, and overall style that aligns with their goals.

- This service can be offered through one-on-one consultations or in group workshops, making it versatile for different client preferences.

Why is this business model lucrative?

- In today's increasingly visual world where first impressions matter more than ever, many people are willing to invest in professional help to improve their appearance.

- With little overhead costs required for this type of business (primarily knowledge and skills), the profit margins can be high.

- Additionally, since word-of-mouth recommendations play a significant role in attracting new clients in the beauty industry, consistently delivering excellent results will ensure a steady stream of customers.

Pet services: Offering pet sitting, dog walking, or grooming services

- Starting a pet service business can be a lucrative venture without requiring a large initial investment.

- Pet owners often struggle to find reliable and trustworthy care for their beloved animals while they are away or busy with other commitments.

- By offering pet sitting, dog walking, or grooming services, entrepreneurs can fill this gap in the market and provide a valuable service to animal lovers.

- Pet sitting: Entrepreneurs can offer pet owners peace of mind by taking care of their pets in the comfort of their own homes. This reduces stress on animals that may not thrive in unfamiliar environments such as boarding facilities.

- Dog walking: Many owners lack sufficient time or energy to exercise their dogs regularly. By offering professional dog walking services, entrepreneurs allow pets to stay active and increase overall wellbeing.

- Grooming services: Regular grooming is essential for maintaining the health and appearance of pets. Entrepreneurs can offer mobile grooming services, saving customers time and ensuring personalized attention for their furry friends.

Launching a pet service business requires minimal upfront costs and has the potential for high client retention rates and repeat business. With proper marketing efforts targeting local neighborhoods and online communities dedicated to pets, entrepreneurs can quickly establish themselves as reputable providers in this thriving industry.

Online tutoring: Providing educational assistance to students remotely

Online tutoring is a lucrative business model that offers valuable educational assistance to students from the comfort of their own homes. With virtual classrooms and video conferencing technology, tutors can connect with students across the globe, eliminating the need for geographical limitations. As more parents and learners seek personalized education solutions, online tutoring presents a cost-effective option that can be started on a shoestring budget.

Benefits of online tutoring include flexible scheduling options for both tutors and students. This allows individuals to tailor their learning experience according to their needs and commitments. Furthermore, online platforms provide access to a wide array of subject areas and specialized tutors who have expertise in specific fields. By offering tailored instruction and personalized attention, online tutors can provide transformative educational experiences for their clients.

Let's take a look at some key advantages of starting an online tutoring business:

1. **Global reach**: The digital nature of this business model enables connecting with students anywhere in the world without being confined by physical proximity.
2. **Cost-effective setup**: Compared to traditional brick-and-mortar establishments, starting an online tutoring business requires minimal overhead costs.
3. **Flexibility**: Tutors can work at times convenient for them while accommodating various time zones; likewise, students can schedule sessions around their other commitments.
4. **Specialized expertise**: Online platforms allow matching each student's unique requirements with highly qualified tutors specialized in specific subjects or areas of study.

With strong demand for accessible education services worldwide, entrepreneurs venturing into the field of online tutoring are well-positioned to make a significant impact while enjoying profitable returns on their investments.

Home cleaning services: Offering professional cleaning services to busy households

Life can get hectic, and maintaining a clean home often gets pushed to the bottom of the priority list. That's where home cleaning services step in - providing reliable and efficient cleaning for households on the go.

With experienced professionals at the helm, these services guarantee thoroughness and attention to detail that busy individuals may not have time for. By hiring a professional cleaner, homeowners can reclaim their weekends and enjoy a spotless living environment without lifting a finger.

Not only does hiring a home cleaning service provide convenience, but it also ensures a healthier living space. These experts use specialized equipment and eco-friendly products to eliminate dirt, dust, allergens, and bacteria that can accumulate over time. With their expertise in tackling even the toughest stains or messes, these professionals deliver exceptional results that exceed expectations.

Why choose a home cleaning service?

1. Time-saving: With demanding schedules becoming increasingly common in today's fast-paced world, many homeowners find it challenging to carve out time for regular housekeeping tasks. Hiring a professional cleaning service takes this burden off their shoulders.
2. Expertise: Professional cleaners are trained extensively in various techniques and methods to provide exceptional results efficiently.
3. Customization: Homeowners can tailor the level of service they need based on their preferences and budget.
4. Peace of mind: Knowing that qualified professionals are taking care of your household chores allows homeowners to focus on other priorities with peace of mind while returning to an immaculate space.

In conclusion, launching your own home cleaning service can be an attractive business opportunity within reach for aspiring entrepreneurs with limited financial resources. The demand for such services is ever-growing as people seek more balance between work and personal life—a venture worth exploring if you're looking for flexibility with potential profitability!

Handmade crafts and products: Selling unique handmade items on online platforms

With the rise of e-commerce, selling handmade crafts and products has become easier than ever. Online platforms such as Etsy, Amazon Handmade, and Shopify provide entrepreneurs with a cost-effective way to showcase their creativity and reach a global customer base.

Benefits of selling handmade crafts online:

1. **Low startup costs:** Starting an online business selling handmade crafts requires minimal investment compared to other business models. All you need is your crafting skills, materials, and a computer with internet access to set up shop.
2. **Flexible work schedule:** Running an online store allows for flexibility in terms of when and where you work. This makes it ideal for those who want to pursue entrepreneurship while managing other responsibilities or commitments.
3. **Access to a vast customer base:** With billions of people browsing the internet every day, selling your handcrafted items through online platforms gives you access to a much larger customer base than traditional brick-and-mortar stores would allow.
4. **Ability to showcase uniqueness:** Handmade items are prized for their uniqueness and personal touch. By showcasing your one-of-a-kind creations online, you can attract customers who appreciate the value of artisanal craftsmanship.
5. **Opportunity for growth:** As your business gains traction and positive reviews from satisfied customers, word-of-mouth recommendations may lead to increased sales and potential collaborations with influencers or retailers interested in stocking your products offline as well.

Whether it's intricately designed jewelry, custom-made clothing or home decor pieces - turning your passion into profit by selling handmade crafts online is an accessible entrepreneurial venture that can blossom into a successful enterprise over time.

Fitness and wellness coaching: Guiding individuals towards a healthier lifestyle

• Fitness and wellness coaching is a lucrative business model that can be launched on a shoestring budget, making it accessible to entrepreneurs who are passionate about health and fitness.

• This business involves providing personalized guidance and support to clients in their journey towards better health. By creating customized exercise plans, offering nutritional advice, and addressing the psychological aspects of wellness, fitness coaches help individuals achieve their fitness goals.

• With the increasing focus on health and well-being, there is a growing demand for qualified fitness coaches. Entrepreneurs with certifications or experience in the field can tap into this market by offering one-on-one coaching sessions, group classes, online programs, or even virtual coaching through video calls or apps. This flexible approach allows coaches to cater to clients with different preferences and lifestyles while keeping costs low.

Don't miss out!

Visit the website below and you can sign up to receive emails whenever Coloring Ape publishes a new book. There's no charge and no obligation.

https://books2read.com/r/B-A-EUZZ-LJUOC

BOOKS 2 READ

Connecting independent readers to independent writers.

Did you love *Monetizing Your Passion: How to Turn Your Hobby into a Lucrative Income Stream*? Then you should read *Email Marketing Mastery: A Hands-On Approach for Small Business Owners*[1] by Coloring Ape!

In today's digital age, email marketing has emerged as one of the most powerful tools for small businesses to connect with their target audience and drive sales. With its ability to reach customers directly in their inbox, email marketing offers a unique opportunity to build relationships, increase brand awareness, and generate valuable leads. In this subchapter, we will delve into the various aspects of email marketing and how it can revolutionize your small business.

First and foremost, we will explore the importance of building an email list. As a small business owner, your email list is your most valuable asset. It consists of individuals who have willingly shared their contact information and expressed interest in your products or services. We will discuss effective strategies to grow your email list organically, ensuring that you reach the right audience and avoid spamming.

---

1. https://books2read.com/u/brB66Y

2. https://books2read.com/u/brB66Y

Next, we will dive into the art of crafting compelling email content. A well-crafted email can grab the attention of your recipients, engage them with valuable information, and motivate them to take action. We will provide practical tips and examples to help you create attention-grabbing subject lines, personalized content, and effective calls-to-action. Whether you are sending promotional emails, newsletters, or automated sequences, mastering the art of email content is crucial for success.

Also by Coloring Ape

Email Marketing Mastery: A Hands-On Approach for Small Business Owners
Monetizing Your Passion: How to Turn Your Hobby into a Lucrative Income
Stream
Vegan Lifestyle for Pregnant Woman
Unleashing the Power of TikTok: Discovering Innovative Ways to Generate
Income on the Platform

www.ingramcontent.com/pod-product-compliance
Lightning Source LLC
Chambersburg PA
CBHW061404140726
47997CB00003B/1354